AlphaBasiCs

Pioneer Life

from A to Z

21956

A Bobbie Kalman Book

Crabtree Publishing Company

www.crabtreebooks.com

AlphaBasiCs

Created by Bobbie Kalman

For John Siemens
and Erika Kilian

Editor-in-Chief
Bobbie Kalman

Managing editor
Lynda Hale

Editors
Niki Walker
Greg Nickles

Photo research
Hannelore Sotzek

Computer design
Lynda Hale
Robert MacGregor

Production coordinator
Hannelore Sotzek

Separations and film
Dot 'n Line Image Inc.
CCS Princeton (cover)

Printer
Worzalla Publishing Company

Special thanks to
Genesee Country Museum; Leigh and Brian Adamson; Sherbrooke Village and the Nova Scotia Museum; Rino Roncadin and Black Creek Pioneer Village, Metro Toronto and Region Conservation Authority; Samantha Crabtree; Upper Canada Village; Toy and Miniature Museum of Kansas City; Fort George

Photographs and reproductions
Marc Crabtree at Black Creek Pioneer Village: page 18 (right)
Marc Crabtree at Genesee Country Museum: pages 6, 17, 20, 31
Marc Crabtree: page 28 (right)
Ken Faris at Upper Canada Village: page 18 (left)
Bobbie Kalman: page 11 (top), 28 (left; at Black Creek Pioneer Village)
Edward Owen/Art Resource, NY: cover, page 13
Sherbrooke Village and the Nova Scotia Museum/Ron Merrick: page 4
Toy and Miniature Museum of Kansas City: page 25 (both)
The Newark Museum/Art Resource, NY: pages 10, 21 (detail)
National Museum of American Art, Washington DC/ Art Resource, NY: page 11 (bottom; detail)

Illustrations
Barbara Bedell: title page, pages 5, 7, 8, 9, 12, 16, 19, 22, 23, 24, 27, 29, 30
Tammy Everts: page 31

Crabtree Publishing Company

PMB 16A
350 Fifth Ave.,
Suite 3308
N.Y., N.Y. 10118

612 Welland Ave.,
St. Catharines,
Ontario, Canada
L2M 5V6

73 Lime Walk
Headington
Oxford OX3 7AD
United Kingdom

Cataloging in Publication Data
Kalman, Bobbie
    Pioneer Life from A to Z

(AlphaBasiCs series)
Includes index.
ISBN 0-86505-376-6 (library bound) ISBN 0-86505-406-1 (pbk.)
This alphabet book introduces various aspects of the pioneer lifestyle in North America, including toys, clothing, school, home crafts, and special occasions.

1. Frontier and pioneer life—North America—Juvenile literature.
2. North America—Social life and customs—Juvenile literature.
3. English language—Alphabet—Juvenile literature. [1. Frontier and pioneer life. 2. Alphabet.] I. Title. II. Series: Kalman, Bobbie. AlphaBasiCs.

E179.5.K355 1997   j973   LC 97-28801
                                                                                      CIP

Contents

is for apples. Apples were important to the pioneers because they were used in many ways. Some apples were eaten fresh and baked in desserts. Others were cored, sliced, and hung to dry above the fireplace. Apples were also made into sauce, cider, and apple-cider vinegar.

Families harvested their apple crop in the fall. Apple-peeling parties were a favorite fall event. People gathered to peel apples, dance, and play a game of bobbing for apples. Part of the crop was stored in the cool, dark cellar so that the apples could be eaten during winter.

is for **bee**. A bee was a work party. It was a fun way to do a big or difficult job. People held bees to sew quilts, husk corn, and build houses. A barn-raising bee is shown below. Neighbors worked together to raise the frame of the barn. The farmer added the walls and roof later.

While the men worked, the women prepared a wonderful meal, and the children played games. People enjoyed going to bees because it gave them a chance to see their neighbors. Most neighbors lived far apart and did not often see one another.

is for **churn**. Pioneers did not buy butter in a grocery store as we do today. They had to make it themselves from cream. Butter was made in a churn, a tall wooden or stone container with a lid. A stick called a **dasher** moved up and down through a hole in the center of the lid.

The young children in a pioneer family usually churned the butter. They rolled the dasher between their hands and pumped it up and down.

1. To make butter, fresh milk was poured into a stone crock. After a day or so, the cream in the milk rose to the top. It was spooned into a clean churn. A child swirled and pumped the dasher.

2. Soon a few clumps of butter formed on the dasher. The butter was ready when clumps of it floated to the top of the liquid. The liquid that did not become butter was called **buttermilk**.

3. The butter was strained from the buttermilk and put into a wooden trough. Water was poured over the butter again and again to wash it. The butter was then pressed with a spatula to squeeze out any water or buttermilk. Salt was added to the butter, and a drop of carrot juice was mixed in to make it yellow. It took about an hour to churn and wash butter.

trough

spatula

butter mold

4. The butter was pressed into a mold to shape and decorate it.

is for **dancing**. Pioneers worked very hard, but they still loved to have fun—and dance! They often danced at home after supper. They danced at bees and held dances called **sprees**. At sprees they did jigs, reels, and **square dances**. A square dance has a **caller** who tells dancers what to do.

Can you call a square dance? Try this one:
Join your hands and circle half—partners swing
Right and left back to the same old thing.

Gents, take your gal—for a promenade.
Stand her by and swing to the next,
Then bring her back with a half gallopade.

is for **ear trumpet**. An ear trumpet was a large metal cone that was used as a hearing aid. Today we have small battery-powered hearing aids that fit into an ear. Pioneers did not have batteries. When people did not hear well, they had to hold an ear trumpet to their ear to catch sounds.

Make your own ear trumpet! Roll a piece of paper into a cone shape. Hold the cone away from your ear and ask a friend to say something. Now hold the cone to your ear and ask your friend to say the same thing into your ear trumpet. Does your friend's voice sound louder?

is for **fashions**. Fashions is another word for clothing. Most pioneer children had only two outfits. They wore one outfit during the week and saved the other for Sundays and special occasions. The "Sunday best" outfit was usually fancier than the everyday outfit.

*Girls wore many layers of petticoats under their dress. The older boy in this picture is wearing a suit with a **waistcoat**, or vest. His pants are shorter than his everyday trousers. The younger boy's suit has a dress instead of a jacket. Young boys wore dresses until they were four or five.*

The word "fashions" also describes clothes that are in style. Wealthy parents dressed their children in the latest fashions. Stylish clothes for children looked like the clothing worn by adults. These outfits were not very comfortable.

Girls did not wear pants until the 1850s, when a woman named Amelia Bloomer made them popular. Pants were called "bloomers" after her. Most girls wore bonnets, which were made of cotton. The dressy bonnet in the top picture was made of straw and cloth.

is for **general store**. Most villages had only one store—the general store. It sold everything the pioneers needed. Few people paid for goods with money. They traded, or **bartered**, butter, eggs, or vegetables for tools, dishes, cotton cloth, coffee, sugar, and spices.

The general store was not just a place to buy and trade goods. People dropped in to chat, play a game of checkers, and hear the latest news from the storekeeper. The post office was located inside the store, so people also stopped there to send and receive mail.

is for **home**. The first home a pioneer family built was a rough, one-room cabin. It was made from logs, mud, and tree bark. Once a town had a sawmill, logs could be cut easily into boards. With boards, a family was able to build a bigger home with two stories and several rooms.

This pioneer home has a wooden floor instead of a dirt one. Bricks cover the hearth. Robert loves playing on the warm bricks. The fireplace provides the family with heat and light. Father watches while Mother spins wool into yarn by the warm glow of the flames.

 is for **illumination**. Illumination is the art of decorating letters with colorful designs. The letters below are illuminated. On rainy days, children illuminated their books. They painted dots, flowers, and curved lines onto capital letters and made borders around the edge of the page.

Look at the examples of illumination on this page. Decorate your stories and projects using these designs or make up some colorful letters of your own.

is for **journal**. A journal is a record of thoughts, feelings, and events that have happened. Many pioneer families kept a journal. It helped them remember jobs they had done together such as clearing land and building their home. Family members also recorded their own experiences.

Monday, July 24, 1865
Today I found a fox near the chicken coop. I picked up my rake and ran towards it yelling. It ran away, carrying a chicken with it.

Father

Tuesday, July 25, 1865
I took my eggs and fresh butter to the general store. I bartered them for a bonnet for Jane.

Mother

Wednesday, July 26, 1865
I wore my new bonnet to school today. Some of the boys even noticed. I felt so good, I won the spelling bee!

Jane

Thursday, July 27, 1865
I went fishing with my buddy Bill and we caught 7 fish. I caught 5 myself but I gave Bill one of mine. Mother made a great fish dinner! Jake

The journal became an important part of a family's history. Your family might enjoy keeping a journal. Start one and have your family members take turns writing in it.

is for **kerosene**. Kerosene is a type of oil that was burned in lamps. The pioneers did not have electricity. They used candles and oil-burning lamps for light. Kerosene lamps burned longer and brighter than candles, and they made less smoke than other oils such as whale or fish oil.

Making candles was a messy job that took hours. A candle's open flame was a fire hazard.

Whale oil was smelly and smoky.

Some kerosene lamps had tin plates that reflected light into the room.

plate

This lamp has a built-in snuffer to put out the flame.

snuffer

*Kerosene lamps, shown above, had a **wick** that could be turned up to give more light. A glass **globe** kept the flame safely inside. Kerosene lamps were both useful and attractive.*

16

is for **livestock**. Livestock, or farm animals, were useful to the pioneers. Work animals such as horses and oxen pulled wagons and plows. Cows and goats gave milk. Meat came from cows, sheep, pigs, and chickens. Chickens also provided eggs. Clothes were made from the hides of animals.

Children fed the livestock every morning. An older child usually cared for the horses. He or she combed them, checked their shoes for stones, and rubbed their tired muscles at the end of the day.

17

is for **mills**. Mills are buildings with machines that do jobs such as grinding grain, sawing logs, or weaving cloth. In pioneer times, mills were powered by wind or water. Many mills were built next to a river, pond, or waterfall. Most villages had two types of mills—a **sawmill** and a **gristmill**.

Grist means "grain." At the gristmill, grains such as wheat and corn were ground into flour or cornmeal. Both were used to make bread, which was a part of every meal. Before there was a gristmill, people had to grind grain by hand. Grinding grain was hard work that made a person's arms ache.

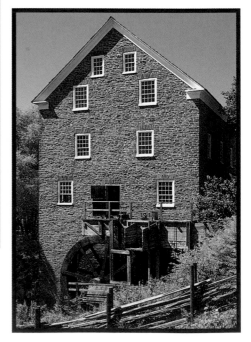

At the sawmill, powerful saws quickly cut huge logs into boards. Before a sawmill was built, people had to saw wood by hand for their houses and furniture.

is for the **New Year**, a special time for the pioneers. On New Year's Eve, church bells chimed, and family members stayed up late to wish one another "Happy New Year." New Year's Day was spent calling on neighbors. People welcomed guests with plenty of food and drink.

*Young men made calling into a contest. They competed to make the most visits. Sometimes they ran in and out of homes in a race to be the winner! At each home they left a **calling card**, a small card with their name printed on it, to prove they had made a visit.*

is for **one-room school**. Pioneer children went to a one-room school. One teacher taught children of all ages. The girls sat on one side of the room and the boys on the other. Parents paid the teacher with food, clothing, and firewood. They took turns boarding the teacher at their home.

*Children were taught the basics—reading, writing, and **arithmetic**, which is simple math. Paper was scarce, so most students did their schoolwork on **slates**. Slates were made of hard rock. Children wrote on them by scratching the surface with slate pencils.*

is for **peddler**. A peddler traveled from village to village selling all kinds of goods. His wagon was like a general store on wheels. The peddler sold pots and pans, clocks, coffee grinders, books, toys, shoes, and cloth. He bartered these goods for homemade candles, soap, quilts, and food.

People were happy to see the peddler because he brought news from other places. Children were especially excited when he arrived. The peddler had toys that they had not seen before. Peddlers often had the latest items from the city. They also sold tonics and other medicines.

is for **quilt**. A quilt is a type of blanket. Pioneer women saved scraps of fabric to make into quilts. They arranged the scraps into a pattern and then stitched them together. This patchwork sheet was the top layer of the quilt. It was sewn onto a wool sheet, and fleece was put between the layers.

*To finish a quilt quickly, women held a **quilting bee**. Several women came to help stitch the layers of the quilt together. After the quilt was finished, the quilters' families joined the women to celebrate with dinner and a party.*

is for **rag rugs**. Rugs became popular in the 1800s, but many people could not afford to buy them. Anyone with worn-out clothing could make a rag rug, however. Women tore old clothes into rags and made them into rugs. The rugs were not only useful, they also brightened up the home.

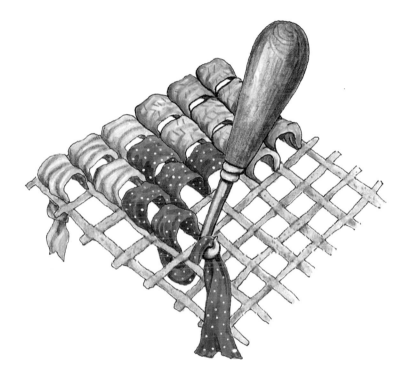

Strips of fabric were hooked onto a piece of burlap to create a thick, patterned rug.

Round or oval rugs were made by braiding the strips into a long braid. The braid was then coiled and stitched.

Square or rectangular rugs could be made by weaving strips together on a loom. In some villages, there was a weaver who wove rugs for others in the community.

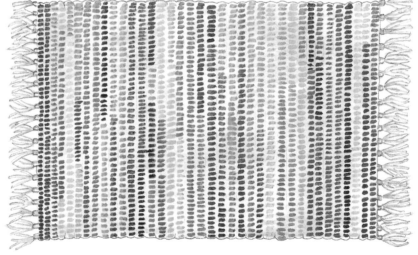

is for **shivaree**. A shivaree, also spelled **charivari**, sometimes interrupted a wedding celebration. Young men, dressed in funny clothes, hats, and masks, went to "serenade" the newlyweds at their home. They made noise with horns, bells, pots, and pans until they were invited to join the party.

A bride or groom was often surprised by shivaree pranks. It was all in good fun, but sometimes the pranksters got carried away! If you were the groom in this picture, would you invite these "musicians" to your wedding party?

is for **toys**. Pioneer children had very few toys, and most of them were handmade. They included hoops, marbles, wooden stilts, and dolls made of rags or cornhusks. Store-bought toys such as board games and china dolls were expensive. They often came from other countries.

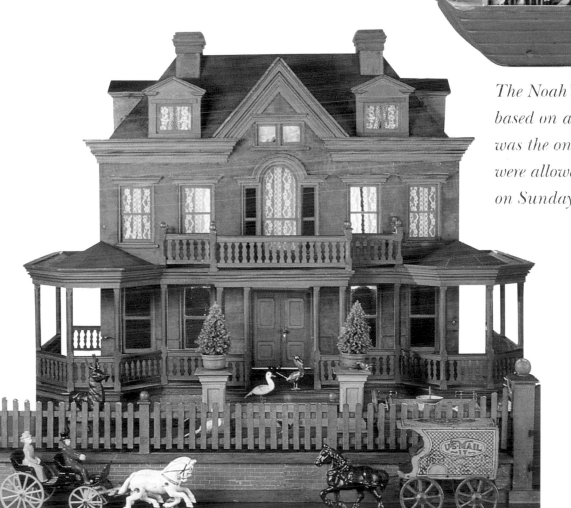

The Noah's Ark toy was based on a Bible story. It was the only toy children were allowed to play with on Sunday.

Dollhouses were filled with tiny furniture that was expensive and easily broken. Most dollhouses were not used as toys. Fathers bought them for their daughters in order to show off their wealth to other people.

is for **undertaker**. An undertaker arranged funerals and prepared people for burial after they died. In many pioneer villages, the carpenter was also the undertaker. He made wooden furniture most of the time, but when needed, he also made coffins.

*The undertaker made coffins from pine. Coffins were plain boxes. They had no padding or decorations. Part of the undertaker's job was to take the coffin to the cemetery on the back of his wagon. For this job, some undertakers had a special wagon called a **hearse**.*

is for **village**. A pioneer village was like a small town. Most had a gristmill, sawmill, general store, schoolhouse, church, and an inn where travelers could sleep. Many farmers lived outside the village. Some lived so far away that they only made a trip to the village once a month.

Tradespeople such as the blacksmith, carpenter, leather worker, and tinsmith offered their services to people in the village and farmers in the area. A doctor, miller, storekeeper, teacher, and printer also worked in a village. This drawing is based on Black Creek Pioneer Village.

is for **wool**. Wool was used to make clothes and blankets. Pioneers did not buy woolen goods in a store. They made them from scratch. Making wool cloth took a lot of time and work. Many people were involved, from the farmer who raised the sheep to the person who wove the cloth.

*This heap of **fleece** will become a new wool blanket. The woman is on her way to wash and comb the fleece before it is spun into yarn.*

Yarn was not only used to weave fabric on a loom. It was also knitted into sweaters, warm mittens, socks, and scarves.

2. Wool was spun into yarn on a spinning wheel. The yarn was then dyed outdoors in a huge iron pot. Dyes added color to the yarn and were made from berries, bark, and vegetables such as onions.

1. After fleece was washed and combed to remove dirt, twigs, and burrs, it was placed between two **carding paddles**. It was pulled through the paddles again and again. Carding fluffed up the fleece so that its fibers were ready to be spun into soft yarn.

3. The dyed yarn was woven into cloth on a loom. The other jobs in making wool were done by the family, but there was often only one or two looms in a village. The weaver was paid either with money or a share of the yarn or fabric.

is for **Xmas**, or Christmas. The letter X stands for the cross, a symbol of the Christian religion. The early settlers celebrated Christmas Day by going to church. By the late 1800s, Christmas had become a week-long holiday. Most people decorated Christmas trees and exchanged presents.

On Christmas Eve, people went on hay rides and told ghost stories by the flickering flames of a fire. Children hung stockings on the fireplace mantel and waited for Santa Claus to fill them with goodies. Caroling was also a popular Christmas custom.

is for **yoke**. A yoke was a wooden bar that rested on an animal's or a person's neck and shoulders. It was used to carry heavy loads.

On most pioneer farms, it was the children's job to fill the animals' troughs with water. This chore took up to 30 trips to the well! A yoke made the water easier to carry.

is for **zoetrope**. A zoetrope was a toy that made pictures seem as if they were moving. A child put a strip of pictures in the zoetrope and then spun it. Looking through the slots on the side, the child watched as the pictures on the strip moved like cartoons.

31

Glossary

blacksmith A tradesperson who makes iron into items such as horseshoes

board (noun) A flat piece of sawed wood; (verb) to give a person meals for pay

caller A person who calls out the instructions in a square dance

carpenter A tradesperson who builds and repairs wooden objects

cellar A room under a building, used to store food and keep it cold

cider The juice pressed from apples

crock A clay or stone jar or pot

fleece The wool of a sheep or goat

hearth A fireplace floor, made of brick or stone

hide The skin of an animal

jig A fast, hopping dance

leather worker A tradesperson who makes leather into items such as saddles and bags

loom A machine used to weave yarn or thread into cloth

needlepoint The art of stitching designs onto cloth with a needle and thread

petticoat A slip worn under a skirt

pioneer (noun) A person who is the first of a group to settle in or explore a land; (adjective) describing things or events relating to early settlers

printer A person who runs a printing press

reel A lively, spinning dance

serenade To sing a song of affection to another person

spree A lively gathering where people dance

square dance A dance in which couples form a square and are told what to do by a caller

Sunday best Describing good clothes worn only to church on Sundays or on special occasions

tinsmith A tradesperson who makes tin objects

tonic A drug or medicine that refreshes or strengthens a person

wick A loosely woven cord that draws up fuel to a flame in a candle or lamp

wool The hair of a sheep or goat; cloth made of this hair

Index

4 5 6 7 8 9 0   Printed in the U.S.A.   6 5 4 3 2 1